Illustrator Man   Idea Lady
Warren Miller   Jeannie McGill

Distributed by The Wine Appreciation Guild
South San Francisco, CA 94080
ISBN # 1-891267-35-3
Printed in Canada
Published by MillGill Publishing, LLC
U.S.A.

A Nose for Wine

BY JEANNIE McGILL

WITH ILLUSTRATIONS BY

Wine is liquid poetry, alluring and provocative — it stirs the mind and soul. Yet too often wine jargon rears its ugly head, manifesting in phrases such as, "This wine is presumptuous yet unassuming, slight yet breathtakingly sleek, with tenderness and spunk." These phrases leave readers scratching their heads and thinking, "Sounds great, but what does it taste like?"

Through the use of clever illustrations, vivid imagery and concise definitions Jeannie McGill and Warren Miller have attempted to disarm the garrulous phrases of wine speak. With a sense of humor and an air of levity, this book aims to slake the reader's thirst to decipher the vocabulary of wine experts. My glass is raised to Mr. Miller and Mrs. McGill for doing just that. Cheers!

Keith Fergel

Keith Fergel, who has been featured in Fortune *magazine, works as a sommelier at the French Laundry (voted "favorite restaurant in the United States) by* Food and Wine *readers.*

I'm Warren Miller and for the last fifty years I've brought you a new feature-length ski film every year. Together with Jeannie McGill I am now bringing you this book about wine and how people try to describe a very complex beverage in a very simple way. From assertive and brambly to unfocused, grassy, smoky, elegant, or chewy, every person who drinks wine has a different set of adjectives to describe what's in his or her glass at the time.

How do you effectively describe wine? Men and women have been trying to do it for the last ten thousand years and there are as many different ways to describe a bottle of squashed grapes as there are ways to describe ski tracks on a sunny powder snow morning.

All I really know about wine is that it comes in two basic colors, red or white, and until they invented the cardboard carton years ago, very few of my friends even thought about drinking it. I only knew four definitions of wine until I started working on this book: red, white, cheap, and expensive. Other than that, I still don't try to describe a glass of wine, other than by saying, "The grapes were grown on a vine, someone picked them, crushed them, and then let them stay in a bottle until the right price came along."

What does it really mean when someone describes wine as tasting like "A rich raspberry with hints of herbaceousness?" Or, "It has a spicy red fruity flavor, with firm tannins and acidity, thus giving it structure?"

"May develop further" can easily be translated by simply turning these pages.

Warren Miller

Rather elegant

a wine that has lively acidity,
velvety texture, persistent finish and
overall pleasing characteristics

Ages beautifully

awaiting to peak — wines lose their harshness
and reach a balance of fruit and acid

Finishes dry

dry sensation (not sweet)
stays with you as you swallow

Voluptuous yet reserved

full-bodied with silky smooth texture but
its aromatic intensity is less than it should be

Explosive in flavor

thickly textured wine which possesses
elevated levels of tastes

A bit woody

the aging on the oak has overwhelmed
the natural fruity taste and smell

Oenology

sometimes spelled enology —
the science of making wine (UC Davis —
a leading institution in the world for that study)

Give it time to open up

giving wine time to aerate — thus
enhancing the flavors

Flute

narrow elongated Champagne glass
that holds bubbles longer

Great legs

after swirling wine in glass, small streams
of wine form down the sides of the glass —
the thicker the leg, the better

Late harvest

wine that is somewhat sweet

Noble rot

same as botrytis, a mold that attacks the
grape and causes it to dehydrate —
this concentrates the flavor and sugar,
making it desirable for dessert wine

Extremely well-balanced

harmony in wine in which none of the
components is overly apparent

Methuselah

equals 8 bottles of Champagne

Full-bodied but lacking in finesse

fullness of feel in the mouth that lacks subtlety —
only the great ones go both ways

Free-run

the juice that runs from the grapes before pressing

Needs time
to settle down

too early to drink

Brut

driest style of Champagne

Well-proportioned

the talents of the wine maker in blending
a wine of very pleasing character

Vertical tasting

tasting the same wine
from multiple years (vintages)

Finishes delicately but lacks backbone

a firm backbone of acidity
is the foundation of all great wine

Full-bodied

fullness of feel in your mouth
due to the thickness of concentrated
wine components and high alcohol

Phylloxera

a root louse or insect that kills the grapevine

Monster yet refined

can't be both astringent or bitter and refined —
beware of the person who describes wine as such

Blind tasting

tasting when the label is hidden

Complex character

scents within scents, tastes within tastes, many
different analogies with fruit, flowers, etc.

Let it breathe

process of aerating red wines —
oxygen usually opens up flavors

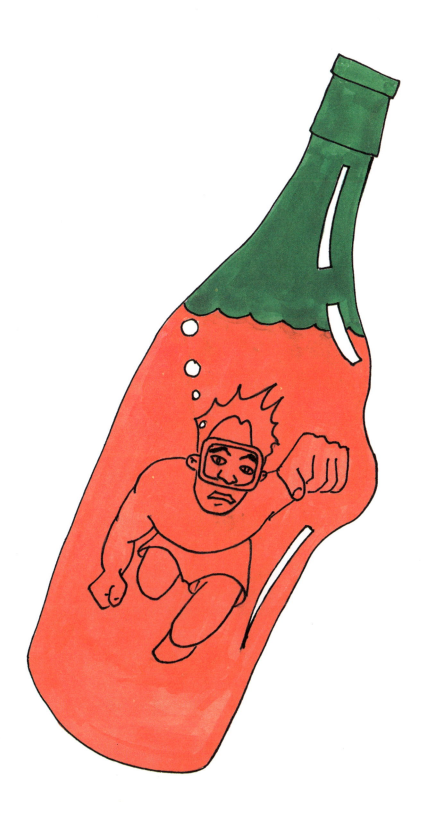

Red of
impressive pedigree

wines that have the best soils and have attained
a high degree of excellence over the years

Jeroboam's connected to the rehoboam

jeroboam = 6 bottles of red or 4 of Champagne
rehoboam = 6 bottles of Champagne

Mature but holding together

complex and subtle — flavors still intact

Sommelier

wine steward
(pronounced as three syllables: "sommel" rhymes with
"pummel" and "ier" sounds like the affirmative "yea")

Starts better
than it finishes

initial taste better than what's in the finish

Magnum

equals 2 bottles of wine

Great nose

describes the bouquet and aroma
of wine — the "greatness" is most associated
with aromatic intensity

Tannin

a natural compound in young reds that
makes you pucker — however it contributes
to the wine's longevity

Barrel tasting

tasting wine that is still aging in the barrel —
Limousin and Nevers are French oaks
widely used for barrel aging

Bouquet

complex nose arising
with maturity in fine wine

Smoooooth

a term better used for scotch or bourbon —
but, in any case, denotes a silky sensation

Shows its age

over the "côte"

Assertive

youthful — the fruit flavors
match the high alcohol

Finishes with a hint of bitterness

a bitter taste that lingers on
the back of your tongue

"One not only drinks wine,
one smells it, observes it, tastes it,
sips it and one talks about it."

EDWARD VII (1841-1910)

Tasting notes

Tasting notes

_____

_____

_____

_____

_____

_____

_____

_____

_____

_____

_____

_____

_____

_____

_____

_____

_____

_____

_____

_____

Tasting notes

_____

_____

_____

_____

_____

_____

_____

_____

_____

_____

_____

_____

_____

_____

_____

_____

_____

_____

_____

_____

_____

_____

Tasting notes

_____

_____

_____

_____

_____

_____

_____

_____

_____

_____

_____

_____

_____

_____

_____

_____

_____

_____

_____

Tasting notes

_____

_____

_____

_____

_____

_____

_____

_____

_____

_____

_____

_____

_____

_____

_____

_____

_____

_____

_____

_____

Tasting notes